Dedicated to a dedicated mother

Denise Roberta Silva-Perez
For always believing me and believing in me.

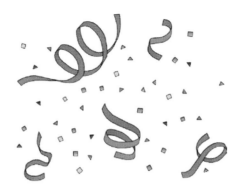

This Book Belongs To

_____

And Has Been Shared With

_____   _____

_____   _____

_____   _____

The
Birthday Suit

Instructions for this book:

Recommended for children as early as age 4.

First read the pages on the right – **black text**.
Read a second time incorporating questions
on the left – grey text.

This will assist in starting an important conversation
with your child about keeping their body safe!

What are babies wearing when they are born?

Nothing! In other words their Birthday Suit.

God made me a
Birthday Suit
with a few
parts for
only me to
see.

Can you point to the parts on your body that need privacy?

Remind your child they always have control of where or how they are touched. It is not just the parts a bathing suit covers.

☑ Arms
☑ Legs
☑ Tummy

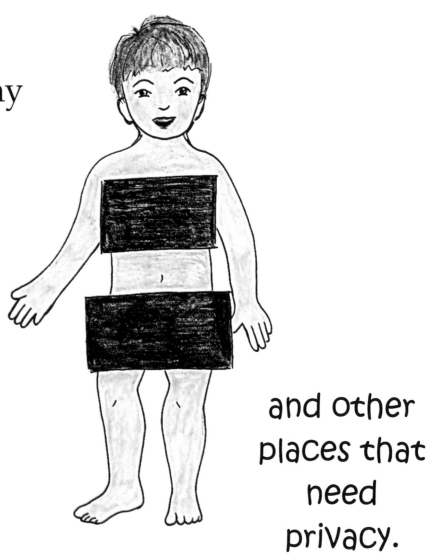

and other places that need privacy.

How long will you have your Birthday Suit?

All your life!

This

suit

grows

with me

and never gets

worn out

or

stained.

Did God make all the suits the same?

No, he made them one by one, unique for every boy and girl.

God did a good job
sewing it on
because it always
fits the same.

Why do we wear clothes?

Warmth, Protection, Modesty

I cover it up
every day
to sleep
and to play,

If someone tries
to mess with it,
I will surely send
them away.

Name the times your whole Birthday Suit is exposed?

Getting Dressed, Changing, Potty, Bath etc.

I will let them know I am able to clean and dress myself.

If I need help,

I'll ask for it...

Thank you very much!

Who can you say no to if you are not comfortable?

Family, Friend or Stranger

I like hugs, tickles and wrestling a bit,

but as soon
as it hurts,
I will demand
that you quit!

Should you tell someone if this happens?

Yes, tell until someone listens!

I can tell them to stop and if they don't obey,

If I need to,

I will RUN

away.

Who made your Birthday Suit?

God

I have to protect my Birthday Suit you see...

someone very special made it for me.

The End

Comments/Questions - Email stewards.ministry@gmail.com

Special Thanks to the Following Children for Feedback

Hailey & Hunter Anderson
Kiely Rose Delaney
Robert & William Incitti
Drake Muldoon
Sophia Naderi
James Perez
Tempe Vakontios
Sarah, Sophia & Andrew Vasquez
Sophia & Olivia Winn

Special Thanks for Support

Messiah Lutheran Church, Yorba Linda

Carlos L. Perez

Lisa & Chris Anderson
Glenn Arthur
Rita Baez
Matt Bagne
Sheila Bates
Rick Beville
Rachel Brito
Svava Brooks
Bobby & Tiffany Campos
Mike Cooke
Diane Cranley
Greg Curley
Michelle Delaney
Jenny Eddings

Ben Muldoon

Barbara Fagins
Diane Farley
Maria Flores
Art Forman
Jane & Bill Oshields Hayner
Alicia Heck
Robert & Elizabeth Incitti
Sue Koches
Suzanne Land
Leslie Lucas
Teri Lyles
Mark & Maria McKenna
Sally & Alex Olea
Romy Orantes

Charley B. Perez

Carmen & Daryl Pease
Sandy Nelson-Perez
Lisa Puccio
Kim Rehm
Keith Rhodes
Neda Riazati
Joanna Roche
Mitch & Shelley Shatzen
Bridgett Silva
Amy Vakontios
Melissa & David Vasquez
Nancy & Bruce Wells
Carrie Winn
Annette Worley

Web References/Resources:

2012

_____

Darkness to Light
www.d2l.org

Erin's Law
http://www.erinmerryn.net/erins-law.html

TAALK - CSA Best Practices
http://www.taalk.org

Child Molestation Prevention
http://www.childmolestationprevention.org

Stop it Now!
www.stopitnow.org

R.A.I.N.N.
http://www.rainn.org

Megan's Law
http://www.megans-law.net

The following information is intended for adults only

There's a bigger reason why the professionals and the courts can't put an end to sexual abuse. They have no permission to talk to a child about sex - unless, of course, they talk to the child after the fact, after the child has already been sexually abused or has abused another child. Only *you* can talk to your children before anything happens, before any damage is done - to anyone.
http://www.childmolestationprevention.org

Author's Prevention Tips:

1. **Know the definition:** Sexual abuse is any contact or interaction (physical, visual, verbal or psychological) between a child/adolescent and an adult when the child/adolescent is being used for the sexual stimulation of the perpetrator or any other person.
   Sexual abuse may be committed by a person under the age of eighteen when that person is either significantly older than the victim or when the abuser is in a position of power or control over the victimized child/adolescent.

2. **Know the statistics:** 1 out of 4 girls and 1 out of 6 boys. 90% of the time it is someone in the family, someone who knows your child well or someone you trust. Socio-economic factors do not change the risk.

3. **Talk to your child:** Have a conversation with your child as early as 4 years old. Why 4? Because this is the time your children become independent and vulnerable to being alone with others. 80% of sexual abuse occurs in a one adult/one child situations. Conversations about their body early on will lay the groundwork for future challenging body topics.

4. **Teach Self-hygiene :** Teach your child self- hygiene and about being mindful of their privacy. Make sure they can wash themselves and dress themselves etc. Children are most vulnerable during the times their body is exposed.

5. **Tell your child what to say and do:** Tell your child what to say. No child molester wants to be found out, teach your child to say "you are not supposed to touch me like that or there". If this happens, encourage your child to keep telling someone until they take action!

Cut this page out if you choose
*See further information on the back.

1 in 4 girls and 1 in 6 boys will be sexually abused before their 18th birthday

That's 20% of our population. The Center for Disease Control estimates that 5-15% of the population will get the flu each year. So next winter, imagine that every person you know who gets the flu was sexually abused as a child and then realize that they represent just a fraction of the people in *your life* who have been affected.

Although it's more comfortable to think of child sexual abuse in terms of "stranger danger," it's a fallacy that child molesters exploit. In fact, child molesters appear most often in our inner circles.

30-40% of the time children are abused by a family member
Another 50% by someone the child knows and trusts

Even if we can accept that abusers are people we know, we tend to hold on to the image of a middle-age man as the typical child molester. While men make-up the largest portion of the population of child molesters, we won't be in a position to truly protect children or effectively support survivors in our lives until we realize that child molesters can also be women and children.

40% of the time the abuser is an older or larger child
8% of abuse happens at the hands of the child's biological mother

Now that we understand how prevalent child sexual abuse is and who child molesters are we are in a better position to protect children. There are over 39 million survivors of child sexual abuse in America and from them experts have documented the signs that appear in children after abuse as well as behavior patterns that appear BEFORE abuse occurs. With the right training, we can recognize when children are in danger and how to put boundaries in place to directly reduce the risk of abuse in our homes, neighborhoods and youth serving organizations.

Child sexual abuse is predictable and preventable
when we surround children with knowledgeable and outspoken adults
and we all play a part in the solution.

Further, now we are in a better position to realize that survivors are not alone. However, keeping the secret and living a lie isolates survivors from God and others and perpetuates self-sabotaging behaviors including trust and intimacy issues, bad boundaries, excessive drug and alcohol use, eating disorders, sexual promiscuity, and even crime. If you are a survivor you understand the impact it can have on your life – emotionally, physically and spiritually, but you are not alone. It was not your fault and you have the power to shift the blame back to where it belongs – on you abuser.

Information Provided by

TAALK
CSA Best Practices
To STOP Child Sexual Abuse

www.taalk.org

To Report Child Abuse

Call **911** or your local Child Protection Services agency or
Call **1-800-4-A-CHILD** if you suspect abuse and need to talk it through.

To Learn Your Part in Preventing Abuse or Find Resources for Healing
Visit www.taalk.org or call **1-888-808-6558**

If You or Someone You Know Struggles with Inappropriate Feelings towards Children
Visit www.stopitnow.org or call **1-888-PREVENT**

Made in the USA
Lexington, KY
25 May 2013